ODE ◆ TO
LONDON
POEMS TO CELEBRATE THE CITY

ODE ◆ TO
LONDON

POEMS TO CELEBRATE THE CITY

EDITED BY
JANE McMORLAND HUNTER

BATSFORD

First published in the United Kingdom in 2012 by

Batsford
10 Southcombe Street
London W 14 0RA
An imprint of Anova Books Ltd

ISBN: 9781849940375

A CIP catalogue record for this book is available from the British Library.

20 19 18 17 16 15 14 13 12
10 9 8 7 6 5 4 3 2 1

Repro by Mission Productions, Hong Kong
Printed by 1010 Printing International Ltd, China

This book can be ordered direct from the publisher at the website:
www.anovabooks.com, or try your local bookshop.

Contents

Introduction

It is difficult to speak adequately, or justly of London.
(The Notebooks of Henry James, 1881)

Everyone knows London, but each one of us will have our own individual thoughts and feelings about the great metropolis. 'The Devil's drawing room', 'The city of the free', 'A shrub among the hills' – ask a hundred people, or a hundred poets, and each will give you a different answer.

There were over three hundred works that could easily have been included in this anthology. There were some obvious choices, but also some surprises. Shakespeare, who lived in London for much of his life, and used the city and its inhabitants for source material rarely mentions it in any detail. Chaucer, who also lived in London, placed his pilgrims at Southwark for the start of their journey, but they are too intent on setting out to really take note of their surroundings. Many of the poets who write about London are actually visitors or immigrants. The earliest poem in this collection is by a visiting Scot, William Dunbar, who extravagantly praises the city, even if his private diaries are less flattering.

Poets' views of London have changed with history. Throughout the Middle Ages and into the seventeenth century people travelled comparatively little and poetry tended to concentrate on valour and love, rather than towns and town life. The early eighteenth century was a time of satire, albeit largely affectionate towards the city, but by the nineteenth century the rural way of life was definitely regarded as superior. Matthew Arnold went so far as to describe the city as 'unpoetic'. The first half of the twentieth century was dominated by the two world wars and their aftermath, influencing poets from D H Lawrence to John Betjeman. The second half brought about further change, and all aspects of London life were debated by locals, visitors and new arrivals alike.

Rather than divide London by area or time, this anthology looks at some of the different aspects of the city, and city life. Without the River Thames London as we know it would probably not exist. For centuries this was the true heart of London; transporting wealth, trade and all manner of people. We may have attempted to harness it with bridges and a barrier, but the river has its own life, a fact recognised by both James Thomson and Carrie Etter, nearly three centuries apart. Grey and dusty as it may seem, London is a green city. Private gardens, street trees, city parks and the wide open spaces beyond the metropolis are as much London as the terraces and tower blocks. London may not be 'small and white, and clean', but one can at least crunch leaves underfoot as winter approaches.

A city is nothing without its inhabitants. Just as important as the millions of people are Eleanor Farjeon's sparrows and T S Eliot's cats. If one believes Imogen Robertson even the statues and paintings are merely slumbering, waiting for a suitable moment to take to the streets again. The famous, the lonely, the busy and the monuments all make up the tangled prints of London's feet. Iconic buildings such as Big Ben and St Pauls are synonymous with the city and often appear in this anthology. But not all buildings have survived and many evolve as the city grows. New structures emerge and places such as the South Bank change, often almost beyond recognition. The pavements, the churches and the miles of suburban houses are all part of London.

The weather is a national obsession in Britain. Each day brings forth a new set of surprises. In recognition of this, the last section of this anthology includes a series of London dawns across the years and seasons.

As this is an *Ode to London* I have unashamedly omitted any poems that I felt did not flatter the city. I have also mostly restricted the poems to those directly about London; one could easily collect another anthology called *Inspired by London*. Where possible I have chosen the version of the poem closest to that which the poet originally wrote. If everything is reduced to an easy read the progress of time is rendered meaningless and much of the beauty and mystery of words is lost.

Jane McMorland Hunter

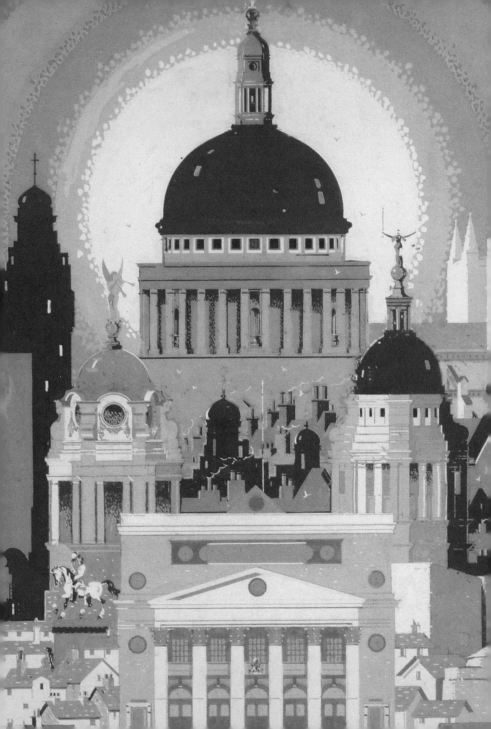

A Mighty
Mass of Brick
and Smoke

———

Arriving at London

from: *Don Juan, Canto X, Verses LXXXI–LXXXIII*

The sun went down, the smoke rose up, as from
    A half-unquench'd volcano, o'er a space
Which well beseem'd the 'Devil's drawing-room,'
    As some have qualified that wondrous place:
But Juan felt, though not approaching *home*,
    As one who, though he were not of the race,
Revered the soil, of those true sons the mother,
Who butcher'd half the earth, and bullied t'other.

A mighty mass of brick, and smoke, and shipping,
    Dirty and dusky, but as wide as eye
Could reach, with here and there a sail just skipping
    In sight, then lost amidst the forestry
Of masts; a wilderness of steeples peeping
    On tiptoe through their sea-coal canopy;
A huge, dun cupola, like a foolscap crown
On a fool's head,—and there is London Town.

But Juan saw not this: each wreath of smoke
    Appear'd to him but as the magic vapour
Of some alchymic furnace, from whence broke
    The wealth of worlds (a wealth of tax and paper):
The gloomy clouds, which o'er it as a yoke
    Are bow'd, and put the sun out like a taper,
Were nothing but the natural atmosphere,
Extremely wholesome, though but rarely clear.

George Gordon, Lord Byron
(1788–1824)

London

Athwart the sky a lowly sigh
　　From west to east the sweet wind carried;
The sun stood high on Primrose Hill;
　　His light in all the city tarried:
The clouds on viewless columns bloomed
Like smouldering lilies unconsumed.

'Oh sweetheart, see! how shadowy,
　　Of some occult magician's rearing,
Or swung in space of heaven's grace
　　Dissolving, dimly reappearing,
Afloat upon ethereal tides
St. Paul's above the city rides!'

A rumour broke through the thin smoke
　　Enwreathing abbey, tower, and palace,
The parks, the squares, the thoroughfares,
　　The million-peopled lanes and alleys,
An ever-muttering prisoned storm,
The heart of London beating warm.

John Davidson
(1857–1909)

The Fire of London

from: *Annus Mirabilis: The Year of Wonders, Verses 215–218*

Such was the Rise of the prodigious fire,
Which in mean Buildings first obscurely bred,
From thence did soon to open Streets aspire,
And straight to Palaces and Temples spread.

The diligence of Trades and noiseful Gain,
And luxury, more late, asleep were laid:
All was the nights, and in her silent reign
No sound the rest of Nature did invade.

In this deep quiet, from what source unknown,
Those seeds of Fire their fatal Birth disclose;
And first, few scatt'ring Sparks about were blown,
Big with the flames that to our Ruin rose.

Then, in some close-pent Room it crept along,
And, smouldering as it went, in silence fed;
Till th' infant Monster, with devouring strong,
Walk'd boldly upright with exalted head.

John Dryden
(1631 – 1700)

On a Bus to Primrose Hill

from: *City Walking I*

Upstairs, in the front seat
of a bus, street and houses
swinging round us, acacia branches
brushing the glass,
I see you: a boy
kicking a stone, playing
on bomb sites, fingering
a stone in your pocket:
looking, feeling the edge
of a concrete building
against softly growing cloud.

*   *   *

You tell me not to look back
until we are high
on Primrose Hill, turning
to see a scattering
of small lights, black
middle distance, and behind,
in a wide arc, towering blocks,
the shell of St.Paul's,
far at the back
Canary Wharf,
a luminous triangle
in the sky.

A greeny grey phosphorescence
in lit windows conceals
unimaginable lives.
Over all, one sound –
a constant hum –
absorbs our words.

Sharp and bright
above petrol dusk
the evening star.

Jeremy Hooker
(1941 –)

London

It is a goodly sight through the clear air,
From Hampstead's heathy height to see at once
England's vast capital in fair expanse,
Towers, belfries, lengthen'd streets, and structures fair.
St. Paul's high dome amidst the vassal bands
Of neighb'ring spires, a regal chieftain stands,
And over fields of ridgy roofs appear,
With distance softly tinted, side by side
In kindred grace, like twain of sisters dear,
The Towers of Westminster, her Abbey's pride;
While, far beyond, the hills of Surrey shine
Through thin soft haze, and show their wavy line.
View'd thus, a goodly sight! but when survey'd
Through denser air when moisten'd winds prevail,
In her grand panoply of smoke array'd,
While clouds aloft in heavy volumes sail,
She is sublime.—She seems a curtain'd gloom
Connecting heaven and earth,—a threat'ning sign
    of doom.
With more than natural height, rear'd in the sky
'Tis then St.Paul's arrests the wondering eye;
The lower parts in swathing mist conceal'd,
The higher through some half-spent shower reveal'd,
So far from earth removed, that well, I trow,
Did not its form man's artful structure show,
It might some lofty alpine peak be deem'd,
The eagle's haunt, with cave and crevice seam'd.
Stretch'd wide on either hand, a rugged screen,
In lurid dimness, nearer streets are seen
Like shoreward billows of a troubled main,

Arrested in their rage. Through drizzly rain,
Cataracts of tawny sheen pour from the skies,
Of furnace smoke black curling columns rise,
And many-tint'd vapours, slowly pass
O'er the wide draping of that pictured mass.

So shows by day this grand imperial town,
And, when o'er all the night's black stole is thrown,
The distant traveller doth with wonder mark
Her luminous canopy athwart the dark,
Cast up, from myriads of lamps that shine
Along her streets in many a starry line:—
He wondering looks from his yet distant road,
And thinks the northern streamers are abroad.
'What hollow sound is that?' approaching near,
The roar of many wheels breaks on his ear.
It is the flood of human life in motion!
It is the voice of a tempestuous ocean!
With sad but pleasing awe his soul is fill'd,
Scarce heaves his breast, and all within is still'd,
As many thoughts and feelings cross his mind,—
Thoughts, mingled, melancholy, undefined,
Of restless, reckless man, and years gone by,
And Time fast wending to Eternity.

Joanna Baillie
(1762 – 1825)

London

I wander thro' each charter'd street,
Near where the charter'd Thames does flow.
And mark in every face I meet
Marks of weakness, marks of woe.

In every cry of every Man,
In every Infant's cry of fear,
In every voice: in every ban,
The mind-forg'd manacles I hear.

How the Chimney-sweeper's cry
Every black'ning Church appalls,
And the hapless Soldiers sigh,
Runs in blood down Palace walls.

But most thro' midnight streets I hear
How the youthful Harlot's curse
Blasts the new born Infant's tear
And blights with plagues the Marriage hearse

William Blake
(1757 – 1827)

To the City of London

London, thou art of townes A *per se.*
 Soveraign of cities, semeliest in sight,
Of high renoun, riches and royaltie;
 Of lordis, barons, and many a goodly knyght;
 Of most delectable lusty ladies bright;
Of famous prelatis in habitis clericall;
 Of merchauntis full of substaunce and myght:
London, thou art the flour of Cities all.

Gladdith anon, thou lusty Troy Novaunt,
 Citie that some tyme cleped was New Troy,
In all the erth, imperiall as thou stant,
 Pryncesse of townes, of pleasure and of joy,
 A richer restith under no Christen roy;
For manly power, with craftis naturall,
 Fourmeth none fairer sith the flode of Noy:
London, thou art the flour of Cities all.

Gemme of all joy, jasper of jocunditie,
 Most myghty carbuncle of vertue and valour;
Strong Troy in vigour and in strenuytie;
 Of royall cities rose and geraflour;
 Empress of townes, exalt in honour;
In beawtie beryng the crone imperiall;
 Swete paradise precelling in pleasure:
London, thow art the floure of Cities all.

Above all ryvers thy Ryver hath renowne,
    Whose beryall stremys, pleasaunt and preclare,
Under thy lusty wallys renneth down,
    Where many a swan doth swymme with wyngis fare;
    Where many a barge doth saile, and row with are,
Where many a ship doth rest with toppe-royall.
        O! towne of townes, patrone and not-compare:
London, thou art the floure of Cities all.

Upon thy lusty Brigge of pylers white
    Been merchauntis full royall to behold;
Upon thy stretis goeth many a semely knyght
    In velvet gownes and cheynes of fyne gold.
    By Julyus Cesar thy Tour founded of old
May be the hous of Mars victoryall,
    Whos artillary with tonge may not be told:
London, thou art the flour of Cities all.

Strong be thy wallis that about thee standis;
    Wise be the people that within the dwellis;
Fresh is thy ryver with his lusty strandis;
    Blith be thy chirches, wele sownyng be thy bellis;
    Rich be thy merchauntis in substaunce that excellis;
Fair be their wives, right lovesom, white and small;
    Clere be thy virgyns, lusty under kellis:
London, thow art the flour of Cities all.

Thy famous Maire, by pryncely governaunce,
    With swerd of Justice the ruleth prudently.
No Lord of Parys, Venyce, or Floraunce
    In dignitye or honour goeth to hym nye.
    He is exampler, loode-ster, and guye;

Principall patrone and roose orygynalle,
    Above all Maires as maister moost worthy:
London, thou art the flour of Cities all.

William Dunbar
(1460– 1520)

The Shadowy Ships of Deptford

The River's Tale

(PREHISTORIC)

Twenty bridges from Tower to Kew –
(Twenty bridges or twenty-two) –
Wanted to know what the River knew,
For they were young, and the Thames was old
And this is the tale that River told:–

'I walk my beat before London Town,
Five hours up and seven down.
Up I go till I end my run
At Tide-end-town, which is Teddington.
Down I come with the mud in my hands
And plaster it over the Maplin Sands.
But I'd have you know that these waters of mine
Were once a branch of the River Rhine,
When hundreds of miles to the East I went
And England was joined to the Continent.

I remember the bat-winged lizard-birds,
The Age of Ice and the mammoth herds,
And the giant tigers that stalked them down

Through Regent's Park into Camden Town.
And I remember like yesterday
The earliest Cockney who came my way,
When he pushed through the forest that lined the Strand
With paint on his face and a club in his hand.
He was death to feather and fin and fur.
He trapped my beavers at Westminster.
He netted my salmon, he hunted my deer,
He killed my heron off Lambeth Pier.
He fought his neighbour with axes and swords,
Flint or bronze, at my upper fords,
While down at Greenwich, for slaves and tin,
The tall Phoenician ships stole in,
And North Sea war-boats, painted and gay,
Flashed like dragon-flies, Erith way;
And Norseman and Negro and Gaul and Greek
Drank with the Britons in Barking Creek,
And life was gay, and the world was new,
And I was a mile across at Kew!
But the Roman came with a heavy hand,
And bridged and roaded and ruled the land,
And the Roman left and the Danes blew in –
And that's where your history-books begin!'

Rudyard Kipling
(1865–1936)

Collecting the Ridges

The skyline geometry and the April fog are again at odds. This prompts me, as usual, to go and stand on Hungerford Bridge to collect ridges of riverwater. Once the commuter exodus has passed, the god of the Thames – for it is too dark to lack a god – goes to his timpani and starts a tremor of sound. I stare harder to hear it. An hour into my work, a group of tourists asks me to take their picture a second time: in the first, they saw nothing they could name.

Carrie Etter
(1969–)

On the Report of a Wooden Bridge to be Built at Westminster

By Rufus' hall, where Thames polluted flows,
Provoked, the Genius of the river rose,
And thus exclaimed: 'Have I, ye British swains,
Have I for ages laved your fertile plains?
Given herds, and flocks, and villages increase,
And fed a richer than the golden fleece?
Have I, ye merchants, with each swelling tide,
Poured Afric's treasure in, and India's pride?
Lent you the fruit of every nation's toil?
Made every climate yours, and every soil?
Yet, pilfered from the poor, by gaming base,
Yet must a wooden bridge my waves disgrace?
Tell not to foreign streams the shameful tale,
And be it published in no Gallic vale.'
He said; and, plunging to his crystal dome,
White o'er his head the circling waters foam.

James Thomson (attributed)
(1700–1748)

Ghosts in Deptford

from: *London Docks*

If ghosts should walk in Deptford, as very well they may,
A man might find the night there more stirring than the day,
Might meet a Russian Tsar there, or see in Spain's despite
Queen Bess ride down to Deptford to dub Sir Francis knight.

And loitering here and yonder, and jostling to and fro,
In every street and alley the sailor-folk would go,
All colours, creeds, and nations, in fashions old and new,
If ghosts should walk in Deptford, as like enough they do.

And there'd be some with pigtails, and some with buckled shoes,
And smocks and caps like pirates that sailors once did use,
And high sea-boots and oilskins and tarry dungaree,
And shoddy suits men sold them when they came fresh from
    the sea.

And there'd be stout old skippers and mates of mighty hand,
And Chinks and swarthy Dagoes, and Yankees lean and tanned,
And many a hairy shellback burned black from Southern skies,
And brassbound young apprentice with boyhood's eager eyes.

And by the river reaches all silver to the moon
You'd hear the shipwrights' hammers beat out a phantom tune,
The caulkers' ghostly mallets rub-dub their faint tattoo –
If ghosts could walk in Deptford, as very like they do.

If ghosts could walk in Deptford, and ships return once more
To every well-known mooring and old familiar shore,
A sight it were to see there, of all fine sights there be,
The shadowy ships of Deptford come crowding in from sea.

Cog, carrack, buss and dromond – pink, pinnace, snake and snow –
Queer rigs of antique fashion that vanished long ago,
With tall and towering fo'c'sles and curving cavern prows,
And gilded great poop lanterns, and scrolled and swelling bows.

The Baltic barque that foundered in last month's North Sea gales,
And last year's lost Cape Horner with wonder on her sails,
Black tramp and stately liner should lie there side by side –
Ay, all should berth together upon that silent tide.

In dock and pond and basin so close the keels should lie
Their hulls should hide the water, their masts make dark the sky,
And through their tangled rigging the netted stars should gleam
Like gold and silver fishes from some celestial stream.

And all their quivering royals and all their singing spars
Should send a ghostly music a-shivering to the stars –
A sound like Norway forests when wintry winds are high,
Or old dead seamen's shanties from great old days gone by, –

Till eastward over Limehouse, on river, dock and slum,
All shot with pearl and crimson the London dawn should come,
And fast at flash of sunrise, and swift at break of day,
The shadowy ships of Deptford should melt like mist away.

Cecily Fox Smith
(1882–1954)

Shadwell Stair

I am the ghost of Shadwell Stair.
　　Along the wharves by the water-house,
　　And through the dripping slaughter-house,
I am the shadow that walks there.

Yet I have flesh both firm and cool,
　　And eyes tumultuous as the gems
　　Of moons and lamps in the lapping Thames
When dusk sails wavering down the pool.

Shuddering the purple street-arc burns
　　Where I watch always; from the banks
　　Dolorously the shipping clanks,
And after me a strange tide turns.

I walk till the stars of London wane
　　And dawn creeps up the Shadwell Stair.
　　But when the growing syrens blare
I with another ghost am lain.

Wilfred Owen
(1893–1918)

Rising Damp

At our feet they lie low,
The little fervent underground
Rivers of London

Effra, Graveney, Falcon, Quaggy,
Wandle, Walbrook, Tyburn, Fleet

Whose names are disfigured,
Frayed, effaced.

These are the Magogs that chewed the clay
To the basin that London nestles in.
These are the currents that chiselled the city,
That washed the clothes and turned the mills,
Where children drank and salmon swam
And wells were holy.

They have gone under.
Boxed, like the magician's assistant.
Buried alive in earth.
Forgotten, like the dead.

They return spectrally after heavy rain,
Confounding suburban gardens. They infiltrate
Chronic bronchitis statistics. A silken
Slur haunts dwellings by shrouded
Watercourses, and is taken
For the footing of the dead.

Being of our world, they will return
(Westbourne, caged at Sloane Square,
Will jack from his box),
Will deluge cellars, detonate manholes,
Plant effluent on our faces,
Sink the city.

Effra, Graveney, Falcon, Quaggy,
Wandle, Walbrook, Tyburn, Fleet

It is the other rivers that lie
Lower, that touch us only in dreams
That never surface. We feel their tug
As a dowser's rod bends to the surface below

Phlegethon, Acheron, Lethe, Styx.

U A Fanthorpe
(1929–2009)

His Teares to *Thamesis*

I send, I send here my supremist kiss
To thee my *silver-footed Thamesis.*
No more shall I reiterate thy Strand,
Whereon so many Stately Structures stand:
Nor in the summers sweeter evenings go,
To bathe in thee (as thousand others doe.)
No more shall I a long thy christall glide,
In Barge (with boughes and rushes beautifi'd)
With soft-smooth Virgins (for our chast disport)
To *Richmond, Kingstone,* and to *Hampton-Court:*
Never againe shall I with Finnie-Ore
Put from, or draw unto the faithfull shore:
And Landing here, or safely Landing there,
Make way to my *Beloved Westminster:*
Or to the *Golden-cheap-side,* where the earth
Of *Julia Herrick* gave to me my Birth.
May all clean *Nimphs* and curious water Dames,
With Swan-like state, flote up and down thy streams:
No drought upon thy wanton waters fall
To make them Leane, and languishing at all.
No ruffling winds come hither to discease
Thy pure and *Silver-wristed Naides.*
Keep up your state ye streams; and as ye spring,
Never make sick your Banks by surfeiting.
Grow young with Tydes, and though I see ye never,
Receive this vow, *so fare-ye-well for ever.*

Robert Herrick
(1591 – 1674)

Trees Freckled in Weak Sunlight

Earthly Paradise

from: *Prologue: The Wanderers*

Forget six counties overhung with smoke,
Forget the snorting steam and piston stroke,
Forget the spreading of the hideous town;
Think rather of the pack-horse on the down,
And dream of London, small and white, and clean,
The clear Thames bordered by its gardens green.

William Morris
(1834–1896)

Twickenham Garden

Blasted with sighs, and surrounded with teares,
    Hither I come to seeke the spring,
    And at mine eyes, and at mine eares,
Recieve such balmes, as else cure every thing;
    But O, selfe traytor, I do bring
The spider love, which transubstantiates all,
    And can convert Manna to gall,
And that this place may thoroughly be thought
    True Paradise, I have the serpent brought.

'Twere wholsomer for mee, that winter did
    Benight the glory of this place,
    And that a grave frost did forbid
These trees to laugh, and mocke mee to my face;
    But that I may not this disgrace
Indure, nor yet leave loving, Love let mee
    Some senslesse peece of this place bee;
Make me a mandrake, so I may groane here,
    Or a stone fountain weeping out my yeare.

Hither with christall vyals, lovers come,
    And take my teares, which are loves wine,
    And try your mistresse Teares at home,
For all are false, that tast not just like mine;
    Alas, hearts do not in eyes shine,
Nor can you more judge womans thoughts by teares,
    Than by her shadow, what she weares.
O perverse sexe, where none is true but shee,
    Who's therefore true, because her truth kills mee.

John Donne
(1572–1631)

London Plane-Tree

Green is the plane-tree in the square,
  The other trees are brown;
They droop and pine for country air;
  The plane-tree loves the town.

Here from my garret-pane, I mark
  The plane-tree bud and blow,
Shed her recuperative bark,
  And spread her shade below.

Among her branches, in and out,
  The city breezes play;
The dun fog wraps her round about;
  Above, the smoke curls gray.

Others the country take for choice,
  And hold the town in scorn;
But she has listened to the voice
  On city breezes borne.

Amy Levy
(1861 – 1889)

London Plane

They felled the plane that broke the pavement slabs.
My next-door neighbour worried for his house.
He said the roots had cracked his bedroom wall.
The Council sent tree-surgeons and he watched.
A thin man in the heat without a shirt.
They started at the top and then worked down.
It took a day with one hour free for lunch.
The trunk was carted off in useful logs.

The stump remained for two weeks after that.
A wren sat on it once.
Then back the tree-men came with their machine.
They chomped the stump and left a square of mud.
All afternoon the street was strewn with bits.
That night the wind got up and blew it bare.

Andrew Motion
(1952–)

Boats on the Round Pond

Destroyers arrowing the water, whose slate
Surface carries the clouds in plastic,
And the surpliced Sunday of October
Lets autumn through the starting gate:

Dogs tear, demons at their back, terriers
Like torpedoes through the long grass; model boats
Throw out their sails like chests, turning
To windward in a morning that floats.

Chaperoning parents, iconoclastic swans, then
Leaves crunched underfoot, the first dead
Crackle of winter; and boat-houses, bandstands
Write Gothic signatures in a sky of lead.

A tanker lies idle at the pond's edge,
Behind it Bayswater soaring with kites,
And rust seems to move on a string
Over trees, freckled in weak sunlight.

Barges, merchantmen, a traffic of cruisers
Make urgent journeys through bruised water,
And eyes are now magnetised by a galleon
Sails matriarchal, a dingy astern like a daughter.

Alan Ross
(1922–2001)

44

Kew Gardens

from: *The Barrel Organ*

Go down to Kew in lilac-time, in lilac-time, in lilac-time.
Go down to Kew in lilac-time (it isn't far from London!),
And you shall wander hand in hand with love in summer's
    wonderland.
Go down to Kew in lilac-time (it isn't far from London!).

The cherry-trees are seas of bloom and soft perfume and sweet
    perfume,
The cherry-trees and seas of bloom (and oh, so near to London!),
And there they say, when dawn is high and all the world's a blaze
    of sky,
The cuckoo, though he's very shy, will sing a song for London.

The Dorian nightingale is rare, and yet they say you'll hear him
    there
At Kew, at Kew in lilac-time (and oh, so near to London!),
The linnet and the throstle, too, and after dark the long halloo
And golden-eyed *tu-whit*, *tu-whoo* of owls that ogle London.

Alfred Noyes
(1880– 1958)

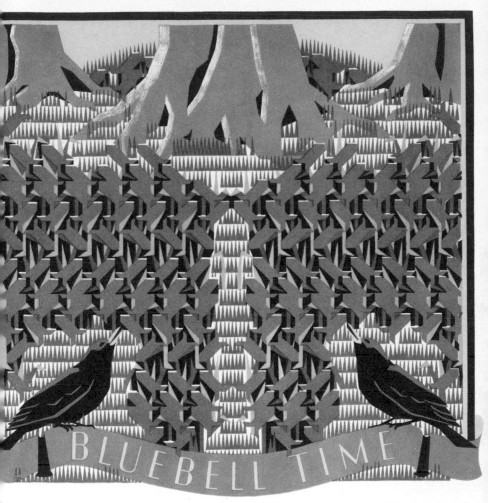

BLUEBELL TIME

IN KEW GARDENS

AND THE **GENERAL** COUNTRY

London versus Epping Forest

The brakes, like young stag's horns, come up in Spring,
And hide the rabbit holes and fox's den;
They crowd about the forest everywhere;
The ling and holly-bush, and woods of beach,
With room enough to walk and search for flowers;
Then look away and see the Kentish heights.
Nature is lofty in her better mood,
She leaves the world and greatness all behind;
Thus London, like a shrub among the hills,
Lies hid and lower than the bushes here.
I could not bear to see the tearing plough
Root up and steal the Forest from the poor,
But leave to Freedom all she loves, untamed,
The Forest walk enjoyed and loved by all!

John Clare
(1793–1864)

The Tangled Prints of London's Feet

The People

Faces, faces in Leicester Square,
Men and women everywhere –
Shop girls, lawyers, tired cashiers,
Housewives, typists, auctioneers.

Thousands and thousands of you there are,
Entered up by a registrar,
Sorted, and checked, and written on forms,
Ready for taxes and war's alarms.

To me you have no name or place,
But only a brief or casual face:
I see you with impersonal eyes
As a flux of furs and various ties.

I see you thus, and yet you go
About my body, to and fro:
Treading the pavement of my mind
Goes the procession of mankind.

Your despair is my distress,
I suffer at your ill-success,
And when you weep, or when you laugh,
I grieve or smile on your behalf.

O faces, faces, hurrying on,
Seen, unrecognized, and gone,
I carry with me from this street
The tangled prints of London's feet!

Clifford Dyment
(1914–1971)

The Londoners

A city is the creation of the human will.
Upon the natural life of the field,
Determined by the radiations of the sun and the swing
    of the seasons,
Man imposes a human space,
A human skyline,
A human time,
A human order.
A city is not a flower.
It does not grow right by itself.
A human creation,
It needs the human powers of intelligence and forethought.
Without them it becomes only a monument to human greed
Out of control, like a malignant tumour,
Stunting and destroying life.

* * *

And the parks and open spaces inside the city:
Battersea Park and Bostall Woods,
Clapham and Tooting Commons,
Peckham Rye and the island gardens of Poplar,
The Regent Canal and the Round Pond of respectable Kensington,
And pram-covered Hampstead.
Areas of light and air where the bands boom on Sunday
afternoons.
Space for strollers,
    Liberty for lovers,
    Room for rest,
Places for play.

* * *

It belongs to them, to make it what they choose.
For democracy means faith in the ordinary man and woman,
    in the decency of average human nature.
Here then in London build the city of the free.

W H Auden
(1907–1973)

Miss Hamilton in London

It would not be true to say she was doing nothing:
She visited several bookshops, spent an hour
In the Victoria and Albert Museum (Indian Section),
And walked carefully through the streets of Kensington
Carrying five mushrooms in a paper bag,
A tin of black pepper, a literary magazine,
And enough money to pay the rent for two weeks.
The sky was cloudy, leaves lay on the pavements.

Nor did she lack human contacts: she spoke
To three shop-assistants and a newsvendor,
And returned the 'Good-night' of a museum attendant.
Arriving home, she wrote a letter to someone
In Canada, as it might be, or in New Zealand,
Listened to the news as she cooked her meal,
And conversed for five minutes with the landlady.
The air was damp with the mist of late autumn.

A full day, and not unrewarding.
Night fell at the usual seasonal hour.
She drew the curtains, switched on the electric fire,
Washed her hair and read until it was dry,
Then went to bed; where, for the hours of darkness,
She lay pierced by thirty black spears
And felt her limbs numb, her eyes burning,
And dark rust carried along her blood.

Fleur Adcock
(1934–)

Bustopher Jones: The Cat About Town

Bustopher Jones is *not* skin and bones –
In fact, he's remarkably fat.
He doesn't haunt pubs – he has eight or nine clubs,
For he's the St James's Street Cat!
He's the Cat we all greet as he walks down the street
In his coat of fastidious black:
No commonplace mousers have such well-cut trousers
Or such an impeccable back.
In the whole of St James's the smartest of names is
The name of this Brummell of Cats:
And we're all of us proud to be nodded or bowed to
By Bustopher Jones in white spats!

His visits are occasional to the *Senior Educational*
And it is against the rules
For any one Cat to belong both to that
And the *Joint Superior Schools.*
For a similar reason, when game is in season
He is found, not at *Fox's,* but *Blimp's;*
But he's frequently seen at the gay *Stage and Screen*
Which is famous for winkles and shrimps.
In the season of venison he gives his ben'son
To the *Pothunter's* succulent bones;
And just before noon's not a moment too soon
To drop in for a drink at the *Drones.*
When he's seen in a hurry there's probably curry
At the *Siamese –* or at the *Glutton;*

If he looks full of gloom then he's lunched at the *Tomb*
On cabbage, rice pudding and mutton.

So, much in this way, passes Bustopher's day –
At one club or another he's found.
It can cause no surprise that under our eyes
He has grown unmistakably round.
He's a twenty-five pounder, or I am a bounder,
And he's putting on weight every day:
But he's so well preserved because he's observed
All his life a routine, so he'll say.
And (to put it in rhyme) 'I shall last out my time'
Is the word of this stoutest of Cats.
It must and it shall be Spring in Pall Mall
While Bustopher Jones wears white spats!

T S Eliot
(1888–1965)

London

To live in London was my young wood-dream,—
London, where all the books come from, the lode
That draws into its centre from all points
The bright steel of the world; where Shakspeare wrote,
And Eastcheap is, with all its memories
Of gossip Quickly, Falstaff, and Prince Hal;
Where are the very stones that Milton trod,
And Johnson, Garrick, Goldsmith, and the rest;
Where even now our Dickens builds a shrine
That pilgrims thro' all time will come to see;
London! whose street names breathe such home to all:
Cheapside, the Strand, Fleet Street, and Ludgate-hill,
Each name a very story in itself.
To live in London! London, the buskin'd stage
Of history, the archive of the past,—
The heart, the centre of the living world!
Wake, dreamer, to your village, and your work.

Robert Leighton
(1822–1869)

UNDERGROUND

THE WAY HOME ALWAYS

KEEPS

LONDON'S

HEART AGLOW

Business Girls

From the geyser ventilators
    Autumn winds are blowing down
On a thousand business women
    Having baths in Camden Town.

Waste pipes chuckle into runnels,
    Steam's escaping here and there,
Morning trains through Camden cutting
    Shake the Crescent and the Square.

Early nip of changeful autumn,
    Dahlias glimpsed through garden doors,
At the back precarious bathrooms
    Jutting out from upper floors;

And behind their frail partitions
    Business women lie and soak,
Seeing through the draughty skylight
    Flying clouds and railway smoke.

Rest you there, poor unbelov'd ones,
    Lap your loneliness in heat.
All too soon the tiny breakfast,
    Trolley-bus and windy street!

John Betjeman
(1906–1984)

65

London Sparrow

Sparrow, you little brown gutter-mouse,
How can I tempt you into the house?
I scatter my crumbs on the window-sill
But down in the gutter you're hopping still:
I strew my cake at the open door,
But you don't seem to know what cake is for!
I drop my cherries where you can see,
I bring you water, I whistle, '*Twee!*' –
But nothing I offer, and nothing I utter
Fetches the sparrow out of the gutter.
What is it makes the road so nice
For sparrows, the little brown gutter-mice?

Eleanor Farjeon
(1881 – 1965)

The Statues of Buckingham Palace

One day, old lion, we will stir ourselves,
shake off the bronze and be flesh.

The sash across my breast is blue I think, my hair
the dirty blonde of your pelt.

First we will look over our shoulders – I'll smile
shyly at the young men who've lounged a century

by the pool, then, without comment, you'll
roll your great shoulders and pad down onto the Mall.

I'll keep my hand warm in the rough tangle
of your mane. We walk past straight-backed generals

dusting the last of the black paint from their coats, while
the gentlemen of state adjust their breeches and steel

swords, clear their throats, and scramble down to the grass.
Along the Embankment we're joined by a few nervous
poets and the occasional nurse. The light is flat, Apollos
blink their olive eyes and begin to tune their lyres;

the muses and graces group with soft calls
to touch each other's pale new skins

with their fingertips. Mythical beasts lope beside us
and the Thames is full of mermaids in pearled scales.

We turn up towards Trafalgar Square, joined
by a Jesus or two, who have clambered

down from the fronts of churches. A little bemused, they rub
their palms and shiver. The military gentlemen give them
overcoats,

clucking under their waxed moustaches. The Jesuses bob
their heads in thanks, feel in the pockets for tobacco.

Then everyone goes to watch as you and I, old lion, climb the
steps
to the Gallery and whisper steeply at the key hole, waking the
pictures.

Imogen Robertson
(1973–)

Towers, Belfries and Structures Fair

Lines and Squares

Whenever I walk in a London street,
I'm ever so careful to watch my feet;
 And I keep in the squares,
 And the masses of bears,
Who wait at the corners all ready to eat
The sillies who tread on the lines of the street,
 Go back to their lairs,
 And I say to them, 'Bears,
Just look how I'm walking in all the squares!'

And the little bears growl to each other, 'He's mine,
As soon as he's silly and steps on a line.'
And some of the bigger bears try to pretend
That they came round the corner to look for a friend;
And they try to pretend that nobody cares
Whether you walk on the lines or the squares.
But only the sillies believe their talk;
It's ever so portant how you walk.
And it's ever so jolly to call out, 'Bears,
Just watch me walking in all the squares!'

A A Milne
(1882 – 1956)

Residence in London

from: *The Prelude 1850, Book VII, lines 119–208*

O, wond'rous power of words, by simple faith
Licensed to take the meaning that we love!
Vauxhall and Ranelagh! I then had heard
Of your green groves, and wilderness of lamps
Dimming the stars, and fireworks magical,
And gorgeous ladies, under splendid domes,
Floating in dance, or warbling high in air
The songs of spirits! Nor had Fancy fed
With less delight upon that other class
Of marvels, broad-day wonders permanent:
The River proudly bridged; the dizzy top
And Whispering Gallery of St Paul's; the tombs
Of Westminster; the Giants of Guildhall;
Bedlam, and those carved maniacs at the gates,
Perpetually recumbent; Statues – man,
And the horse under him – in gilded pomp
Adorning flowery gardens, 'mid vast squares;
The Monument, and that Chamber of the Tower
Where England's sovereigns sit in long array,
Their steeds bestriding, – every mimic shape
Cased in the gleaming mail the monarch wore,
Whether for gorgeous tournament addressed,
Or life and death upon the battlefield.
Those bold imaginations in due time
Had vanished, leaving others in their stead:
And now I looked upon the living scene;
Familiarly perused it; oftentimes,
In spite of strong disappointment, pleased

Through courteous self-submission, as a tax
Paid to the object by prescriptive right.

Rise up, thou monstrous ant-hill on the plain
Of a too busy world! Before me flow,
Thou endless stream of men and moving things!
Thy every-day appearance, as it strikes –
With wonder heightened, or sublimed by awe –
On strangers, of all ages; the quick dance
Of colours, lights, and forms; the deafening din;
The comers and the goers face to face,
Face after face; the string of dazzling wares,
Shop after shop, with symbols, blazoned names,
And all the tradesmen's honours overhead:
Here, fronts of houses, like a title-page
With letters huge inscribed from top to toe;
Stationed above the door, like guardian saints,
There, allegoric shapes, female or male,
Or physiognomies of real men,
Land-warriors, kings, admirals of the sea,
Boyle, Shakespeare, Newton, or the attractive head
Of some quack-doctor, famous in his day.

Meanwhile the roar continues, till at length,
Escaped as from an enemy, we turn
Abruptly into some sequestered nook,
Still as a sheltered place when the winds blow loud!
At leisure, thence, through tracts of thin resort,
And sights and sounds that come at intervals,
We take our way. A raree-show is here,
With children gathered round; another street
Presents a company of dancing dogs,
Or dromedary, with an antic pair

Of monkeys on his back; a minstrel band
Of Savoyards; or, single and alone,
An English ballad-singer. Private courts,
Gloomy as coffins, and unsightly lanes
Thrilled by some female vendor's scream, belike
The very shrillest of all London cries,
May then entangle our impatient steps;
Conducted through those labyrinths, unawares,
To privileged regions and inviolate,
Where from their airy lodges studious lawyers
Look out on waters, walks and gardens green.

　　Thence back into the throng, until we reach,
Following the tide that slackens by degrees,
Some half-frequented scene, where wider streets
Bring straggling breezes of suburban air.

William Wordsworth
(1770–1856)

Suburban Villas

from: *Retirement, lines 481–500*

Suburban villas, highway-side retreats,
That dread th'encroachment of our growing streets,
Tight boxes, neatly sash'd, and in a blaze
With all a July sun's collected rays,
Delight the citizen, who gasping there,
Breathes clouds of dust, and calls it country air.
O sweet retirement, who would balk the thought,
That could afford retirement, or could not?
'Tis such an easy walk, so smooth and straight,
The second milestone fronts the garden gate;
A step if fair, and, if a shower approach,
You find safe shelter in the next stage-coach.
There, prison'd in a parlour snug and small,
Like bottled wasps upon a southern wall,
The man of bus'ness and his friends compress'd,
Forget their labours, and yet find no rest;
But still 'tis rural,—trees are to be seen
From ev'ry window, and the fields are green;
Ducks paddle in the pond before the door,
And what could a remoter scene show more?

William Cowper
(1731 – 1800)

The South Bank

Where the seagulls congregate for symphonies
a stone's throw from Mandela's profile

Where a living parrot once graced a gallery
but backed her feathers to the avant style
and even caused controversy

Where many elderly meet for warmth and tea and cake
and skateboarders were delinquent swans on a concrete lake

Where foyer music is free to all
whether your ear be chamber-tuned, orchestral, jazzy

Where a little walk across a hall
leads you to visual arts and living crafts
for does not driftwood sculpture come from a breathing sea?

Where at summer's freeing heights
a blitz of dance transforms a floor
to tap ballet kathak and more

Where a poetry library awaits you
with diverse verse from epic to haiku

Gone the days when winding walkways
formed an up and down maze
As a new piazza invites a river view
And ground-level entrances embrace a complex venue.

Walk in and be entranced. Do.

John Agard
(1949–)

Oranges and Lemons

Oranges and lemons,
Say the bells of St. Clement's.

You owe me five farthings,
Say the bells of St. Martin's.

When will you pay me?
Say the bells of Old Bailey.

When I grow rich,
Say the bells of Shoreditch.

When will that be?
Say the bells of Stepney.

I do not know,
Says the great bell at Bow.

Here comes a candle to light you to bed,
Here comes a chopper to chop off your head!

Traditional Nursery Rhyme

Holy Smoke

I am the Vicar of St Paul's
And I'm ringing the steeple bell,
The floor of the church is on fire,
Or the lid has come off hell.

Shall I ring the fire brigade?
Or should I trust the Lord?
Oh dear! I've just remembered,
I don't think we're insured!

'What's this then?' said the fire-chief.
'Is this church C of E?
It is? Then we can't put it out,
My lads are all RC!'

Spike Milligan
(1918–2002)

The Mermaid

from: *A Letter to Ben Jonson*

Methinks the little wit I had is lost
Since I last saw you, for wit is like a rest
Held up at Tennis, which men doe the best,
With the best gamesters: What things have we seen,
Done at the Mermaid! heard words that have been
So nimble, and so full of subtill flame,
As if that every one from whence they came,
Had meant to put his whole wit in a jest,
And had resolv'd to live a foole, the rest
Of his dull life; then when there hath been throwne
Wit able enough to justifie the Towne
For three dayes past, wit that might warrant be
For the whole City to talk foolishly
Till that were cancel'd, and when that was gone,
We left an aire behind us, which alone,
Was able to make the two next companies
Right witty; though but downright fools, more wise.

Francis Beaumont
(1584–1616)

To Paint the Summer Morning

———

London's Summer Morning

Who has not wak'd to list the busy sounds
Of summer's morning, in the sultry smoke
Of noisy London? On the pavement hot
The sooty chimney-boy, with dingy face
And tatter'd covering, shrilly bawls his trade,
Rousing the sleepy housemaid. At the door
The milk-pail rattles, and the tinkling bell
Proclaims the dustman's office; while the street
Is lost in clouds impervious. Now begins
The din of hackney-coaches, waggons, carts;
While tinmen's shops, and noisy trunk-makers,
Knife-grinders, coopers, squeaking cork-cutters,
Fruit-barrows, and the hunger-giving cries
Of vegetable-vendors, fill the air.
Now ev'ry shop displays its varied trade,
And the fresh-sprinkled pavement cools the feet
Of early walkers. At the private door
The ruddy housemaid twirls the busy mop,
Annoying the smart 'prentice, or neat girl,
Tripping with band-box lightly. Now the sun
Darts burning splendour on the glitt'ring pane,
Save where the canvas awning throws a shade
On the gay merchandize. Now, spruce and trim,
In shops (where beauty smiles with industry,)
Sits the smart damsel; while the passenger
Peeps thro' the window, watching ev'ry charm.
Now pastry dainties catch the eye minute
Of humming insects, while the limy snare

Waits to enthrall them. Now the lamp-lighter
Mounts the tall ladder, nimbly vent'rous,
To trim the half-filled lamp; while at his feet
The pot-boy yells discordant! All along
The sultry pavement, the old-clothes-man cries
In tone monotonous, while side-long views
The area for his traffic: now the bag
Is slyly opened, and the half-worn suit
(Sometimes the pilfer'd treasure of the base
Domestic spoiler), for one half its worth,
Sinks in the green abyss. The porter now
Bears his huge load along the burning way;
And the poor poet wakes from busy dreams,
To paint the summer morning.

Mary Robinson
(1758–1800)

Composed Upon Westminster Bridge

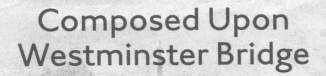

September 3, 1802
Written on the roof of a coach, on my way to France.

Earth has not anything to show more fair:
Dull would he be of soul who could pass by
A sight so touching in its majesty:
This City now doth, like a garment, wear
The beauty of the morning; silent, bare,
Ships, towers, domes, theatres, and temples lie
Open unto the fields, and to the sky;

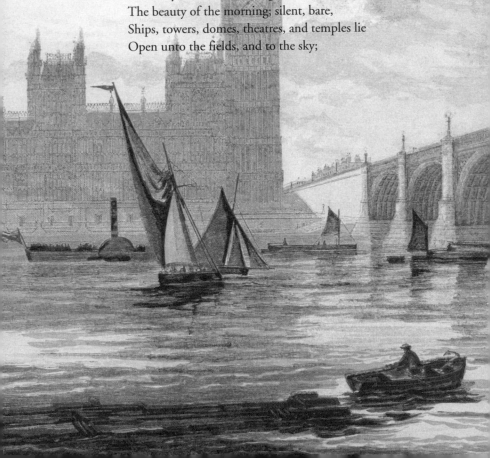

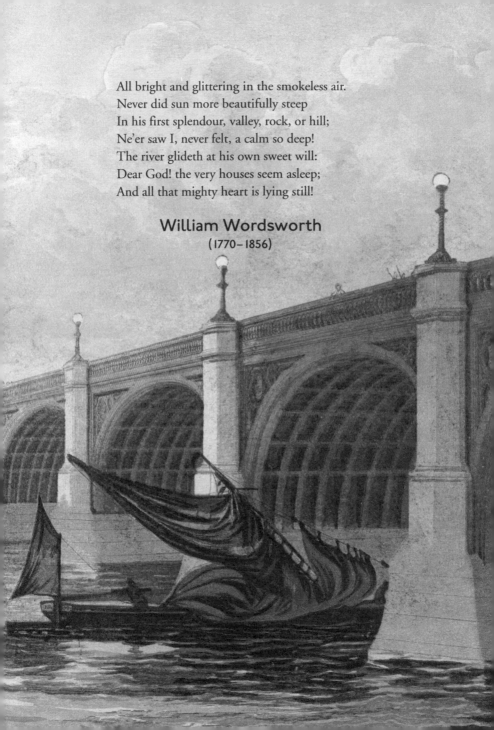

All bright and glittering in the smokeless air.
Never did sun more beautifully steep
In his first splendour, valley, rock, or hill;
Ne'er saw I, never felt, a calm so deep!
The river glideth at his own sweet will:
Dear God! the very houses seem asleep;
And all that mighty heart is lying still!

William Wordsworth
(1770–1856)

London Snow

When men were all asleep the snow came flying,
In large white flakes falling on the city brown,
Stealthily and perpetually settling and loosely lying,
    Hushing the latest traffic of the drowsy town;
Deadening, muffling, stifling its murmurs failing;
Lazily and incessantly floating down and down:
    Silently sifting and veiling road, roof and railing;
Hiding difference, making unevenness even,
Into angles and crevices softly drifting and sailing.
    All night it fell, and when full inches seven
It lay in the depth of its uncompacted lightness,
The clouds blew off from a high and frosty heaven;
    And all woke earlier for the unaccustomed brightness
Of the winter dawning, the strange unheavenly glare:
The eye marvelled—marvelled at the dazzling whiteness;
    The ear hearkened to the stillness of the solemn air;
No sound of wheel rumbling nor of foot falling,
And the busy morning cries came thin and spare.
    Then boys I heard, as they went to school, calling,
They gathered up the crystal manna to freeze
Their tongues with tasting, their hands with snowballing;
    Or rioted in a drift, plunging up to the knees;
Or peering up from under the white-mossed wonder,
'O look at the trees!' they cried, 'O look at the trees!'
    With lessened load a few carts creak and blunder,
Following along the white deserted way,
A country company long dispersed asunder:
    When now already the sun, in pale display
Standing by Paul's high dome, spread forth below

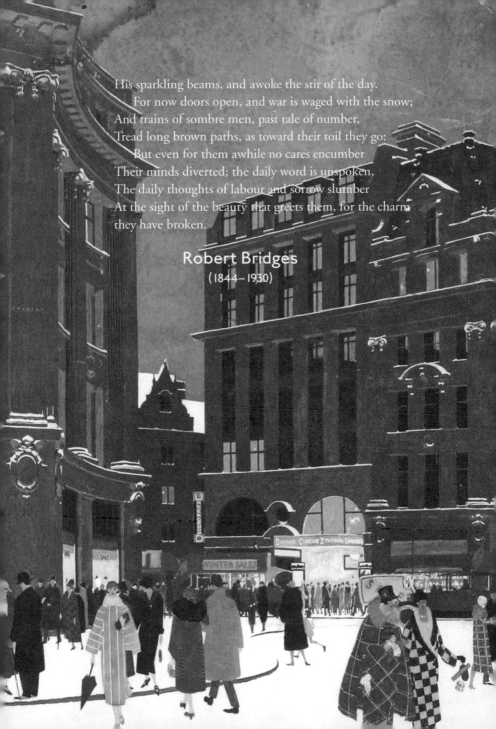

His sparkling beams, and awoke the stir of the day.
    For now doors open, and war is waged with the snow;
And trains of sombre men, past tale of number,
Tread long brown paths, as toward their toil they go:
    But even for them awhile no cares encumber
Their minds diverted; the daily word is unspoken,
The daily thoughts of labour and sorrow slumber
At the sight of the beauty that greets them, for the charm
they have broken.

Robert Bridges
(1844–1930)

Fog

Magically awakened to a strange, brown night
The streets lie cold. A hush of heavy gloom
Dulls the noise of the wheels to a murmur dead:
Near and sudden the passing figures loom;
And out of the darkness steep on startled sight
The topless walls in apparition emerge.
Nothing revealing but their own thin flames,
The rayless lamps burn faint and bleared and red:
Link-boys' cries, and the shuffle of horses led,
Pierce the thick air; and like a distant dirge,
Melancholy horns wail from the shrouded Thames.
Long the blind morning hooded the dumb town;
Till lo! in an instant winds arose, and the air
Lifted: at once, from a cold and spectral sky
Appears the sun, and laughs in a mockery down
On the groping travellers far from where they deem,
In unconjectured roads; the dwindled stream
Of traffic in slow confusion crawling by:
The baffled hive of helpless man laid bare.

Lawrence Binyon
(1869– 1943)

Leaving

from: *Rhymes on the Road, extracted from the Journal of a Travelling Member of the Poco-Curante Society, 1819*

Go where we may – rest where we will,
Eternal London haunts us still.

Thomas Moore
(1779–1852)

Index to Poets

Acknowledgements

Fleur Adcock, 'Miss Hamilton in London' from *Tigers*, Oxford University Press (1967). Reproduced with kind permission of Bloodaxe Books.

John Agard, 'The South Bank' from *A Stone's Throw from Embankment*, Royal Festival Hall (1993). Reproduced with kind permission of Bloodaxe Books.

WH Auden, 'Londoners' from *The Complete Works of WH Auden: WH Auden and Christopher Isherwood: Plays 1928–1938*, Faber & Faber (1989). Reproduced with kind permission of Faber & Faber.

John Betjeman, 'Business Girls' from *John Betjeman's Collected Poems*, John Murray (1958). Reproduced with kind permission of John Murray Publishers.

Laurence Binyon, 'Fog' from *Collected Poems Of Laurence Binyon: London Visions, Narrative Poems & Translations*, MacMillan (1931). Reproduced with kind permission of the Society of Authors.

Clifford Dyment, 'People' from *Collected Poems of Clifford Dyment*, JM Dent & Sons (1970). Reproduced with kind permission of Hachette Livre.

TS Eliot, 'Bustopher Jones' from *Old Possum's Book of Practical Cats*, Faber & Faber (1939). Reproduced with kind permission of Faber & Faber.

Carrie Etter, 'Collecting the Ridges' from *The Tethers*, Seren: Poetry Press Wales (2009). Reproduced with kind permission of Carrie Etter.

UA Fanthorpe, 'Rising Damp' from *U A Fanthorpe: New and Collected Poems,* Enitharmon Press (2010). Reproduced with kind permission of U A Fanthorpe & Dr R V Bailey.

Eleanor Farjeon, 'London Sparrow' from *Silver-Sand and Snow*, Michael Joseph (1951). Reproduced with kind permission of David Higham Associates.

Jeremy Hooker, 'On a bus to Primrose Hill' from *The Cut of the Light: Poems 1965 – 2005*, Enitharmon Press (2006). Reproduced with kind permission of Enitharmon Press.

Spike Milligan, 'Holy Smoke' from *A Book of Bits or a Bit of a Book*, Dobson Books (1965). Reproduced by kind permission of Spike Milligan Productions.

AA Milne, 'Lines and Squares' from *When We Were Very Young*, Metheun (1924). Reproduced by kind permission of Egmont.

Andrew Motion, 'London Plane' from *The Cinder Path*, Faber & Faber (2009). Reproduced with kind permission of Faber & Faber.

Alfred Noyes, 'Kew Gardens' from *The Collected Poems of Alfred Noyes*, John Murray (1950). Reproduced with kind permission of John Murray Publishers.

Imogen Robertson, 'The Statues of Buckingham Palace' from *City State*, Penned in the Margins (2009). Reproduced by kind permission of Imogen Robertson.

Alan Ross, 'Boats on the Round Pond' from *Something of the Sea: Poems 1942–1952*, Derek Verschoyle (1954). Reproduced with kind permission of Carlton Books.

Anova Books is committed to respecting the intellectual property rights of others. We have therefore taken all reasonable efforts to ensure that the reproduction of all contents on these pages is done with the full consent of the copyright owners. If you are aware of unintentional omissions, please contact the company directly so that any necessary corrections may be made for future editions.

Picture Credits

Editor's Acknowledgements

I would like to thank Lucy Smith and Nicola Newman at Batsford and, as always, my agent Teresa Chris. Much of my research was done at the Saison Poetry Library at the Royal Festival Hall. Set in the heart of London, overlooking the Thames, this library has an amazing collection of books, fantastic resources online, wonderfully helpful staff and is a joy to use. Many people helped me with suggestions of poems, in particular, thanks to David and Louy Piachaud for getting me started. Thanks also to Aimi Engineer and Tony Smith at Slightly Foxed for their organisation, help and tolerance. Most of all, though, huge thanks to David Gibb for finding poets and poems and, together with Louy, forcing me to be ruthless when it came to choosing.